FRANCIS FRITH'S

AROUND PENARTH

PHOTOGRAPHIC MEMORIES

MARK ISAACS lives in the Roath area of Cardiff with his wife and young son. Working for Cardiff Libraries for the past 16 years has allowed him to indulge his interest in both books and local history. He is a passionate collector of vintage magazines and records. When not immersed in all this paper and vinyl he follows the fortunes of Cardiff City Football Club. This is his second book for The Francis Frith Collection, following 'Cardiff Old and New'. It is respectfully dedicated to the staff of Llandough Hospital where his son was born and his father was recently cared for so well.

FRANCIS FRITH'S
PHOTOGRAPHIC MEMORIES

AROUND PENARTH

PHOTOGRAPHIC MEMORIES

MARK ISAACS

First published in the United Kingdom in 2005 by The
Francis Frith Collection®

Hardback edition 2005 ISBN 1-84589-025-6

Paperback edition 2005 ISBN 1-84589-020-5

Text and Design copyright The Francis Frith Collection®
Photographs copyright The Francis Frith Collection®
except where indicated.

The Frith® photographs and the Frith® logo are reproduced under
licence from Heritage Photographic Resources Ltd, the owners of the
Frith® archive and trademarks.
'The Francis Frith Collection', 'Francis Frith' and 'Frith' are registered
trademarks of Heritage Photographic Resources Ltd.

All rights reserved. No photograph in this publication may be sold to
a third party other than in the original form of this publication,
or framed for sale to a third party. No parts of this publication may be
reproduced, stored in a retrieval system, or transmitted, in any form,
or by any means, electronic, mechanical, photocopying, recording
or otherwise, without the prior permission of the publishers and
copyright holder.

British Library Cataloguing in Publication Data

Around Penarth - Photographic Memories
Mark Isaacs

The Francis Frith Collection
Frith's Barn, Teffont,
Salisbury, Wiltshire SP3 5QP
Tel: +44 (0) 1722 716 376
Email: info@francisfrith.co.uk
www.francisfrith.co.uk

Printed and bound in Great Britain

Front Cover: **PENARTH**, *The Pier 1896* 38464t
Frontispiece: **PENARTH**, *St Augustine's Church
            1896* 38720

*The colour-tinting is for illustrative purposes only, and is not intended
to be historically accurate*

Aerial photographs reproduced under licence from
Simmons Aerofilms Limited.
Historical Ordnance Survey maps reproduced under licence from
Homecheck.co.uk
Every attempt has been made to contact copyright holders of
illustrative material. We will be happy to give full acknowledgement
in future editions for any items not credited. Any information should
be directed to The Francis Frith Collection.

AS WITH ANY HISTORICAL DATABASE THE FRITH ARCHIVE IS
CONSTANTLY BEING CORRECTED AND IMPROVED AND THE
PUBLISHERS WOULD WELCOME INFORMATION ON OMISSIONS
OR INACCURACIES

CONTENTS

FRANCIS FRITH: VICTORIAN PIONEER	7
AROUND PENARTH - AN INTRODUCTION	10
PENARTH	15
PENARTH FROM THE AIR	56
LLANDOUGH AND SULLY	58
ORDNANCE SURVEY MAP	64
LAVERNOCK AND SWANBRIDGE	66
PENARTH FROM THE AIR	74
DINAS POWIS	76
COUNTY MAP	82
ST FAGANS, ST NICHOLAS AND WENVOE	84
INDEX	89
NAMES OF PRE-PUBLICATION BUYERS	90
Free Mounted Print Voucher	93

FRANCIS FRITH
VICTORIAN PIONEER

FRANCIS FRITH, founder of the world-famous photographic archive, was a complex and multi-talented man. A devout Quaker and a highly successful Victorian businessman, he was philosophical by nature and pioneering in outlook.

By 1855 he had already established a wholesale grocery business in Liverpool, and sold it for the astonishing sum of £200,000, which is the equivalent today of over £15,000,000. Now a very rich man, he was able to indulge his passion for travel. As a child he had pored over travel books written by early explorers, and his fancy and imagination had been stirred by family holidays to the sublime mountain regions of Wales and Scotland. 'What lands of spirit-stirring and enriching scenes and places!' he had written. He was to return to these scenes of grandeur in later years to 'recapture the thousands of vivid and tender memories', but with a different purpose. Now in his thirties, and captivated by the new science of photography, Frith set out on a series of pioneering journeys up the Nile and to the Near East that occupied him from 1856 until 1860.

INTRIGUE AND EXPLORATION

These far-flung journeys were packed with intrigue and adventure. In his life story, written when he was sixty-three, Frith tells of being held captive by bandits, and of fighting 'an awful midnight battle to the very point of surrender with a deadly pack of hungry, wild dogs'. Wearing flowing Arab costume, Frith arrived at Akaba by camel sixty years before Lawrence of Arabia, where he encountered 'desert princes and rival sheikhs, blazing with jewel-hilted swords'.

He was the first photographer to venture beyond the sixth cataract of the Nile. Africa was still the mysterious 'Dark Continent', and Stanley and Livingstone's historic meeting was a decade into the future. The conditions for picture taking confound belief. He laboured for hours in his wicker dark-room in the sweltering heat of the desert, while the volatile chemicals fizzed dangerously in their trays. Back in London he exhibited his photographs and was 'rapturously cheered' by members of the Royal Society. His reputation as a photographer was made overnight.

VENTURE OF A LIFE-TIME

Characteristically, Frith quickly spotted the opportunity to create a new business as a specialist publisher of photographs. He lived in an era of immense and sometimes violent change.

For the poor in the early part of Victoria's reign work was exhausting and the hours long, and people had precious little free time to enjoy themselves. Most had no transport other than a cart or gig at their disposal, and rarely travelled far beyond the boundaries of their own town or village. However, by the 1870s the railways had threaded their way across the country, and Bank Holidays and half-day Saturdays had been made obligatory by Act of Parliament. All of a sudden the working man and his family were able to enjoy days out and see a little more of the world.

With typical business acumen, Francis Frith foresaw that these new tourists would enjoy having souvenirs to commemorate their days out. In 1860 he married Mary Ann Rosling and set out on a new career: his aim was to photograph every city, town and village in Britain. For the next thirty years he travelled the country by train and by pony and trap, producing fine photographs of seaside resorts and beauty spots that were keenly bought by millions of Victorians. These prints were painstakingly pasted into family albums and pored over during the dark nights of winter, rekindling precious memories of summer excursions.

THE RISE OF FRITH & CO

Frith's studio was soon supplying retail shops all over the country. To meet the demand he gathered about him a small team of photographers, and published the work of independent artist-photographers of the calibre of Roger Fenton and Francis Bedford. In order to gain some understanding of the scale of Frith's business one only has to look at the catalogue issued by Frith & Co in 1886: it runs to some 670 pages, listing not only many thousands of views of the British Isles but also many photographs of most European countries, and China, Japan, the USA and Canada - note the sample page shown on page 9 from the hand-written Frith & Co ledgers recording the pictures. By 1890 Frith had created the greatest specialist photographic publishing company in the world, with over 2,000 sales outlets - more than the combined number that Boots and WH Smith have today! The picture on the next page shows the Frith & Co display board at Ingleton in the Yorkshire Dales (left of window). Beautifully constructed with a mahogany frame and gilt inserts, it could display up to a dozen local scenes.

POSTCARD BONANZA

The ever-popular holiday postcard we know today took many years to develop. In 1870 the Post Office issued the first plain cards, with a pre-printed stamp on one face. In 1894 they allowed other publishers' cards to be sent through the mail with an attached adhesive halfpenny stamp. Demand grew rapidly, and in 1895 a new size of postcard was permitted called the court card, but there was little room for illustration. In 1899, a year after Frith's death, a new card measuring 5.5 x 3.5 inches became the standard format, but it was not until 1902 that the divided back came into being, so that the address and message could be on one face and a full-size illustration on the other. Frith & Co were in the vanguard of postcard development: Frith's sons Eustace and Cyril continued their father's monumental task, expanding the number of views offered to the public and recording more and more places in Britain, as the coasts and countryside were opened up to mass travel.

Francis Frith had died in 1898 at his villa in Cannes, his great project still growing. The archive he created continued in business for another seventy years. By 1970 it contained over a third of a million pictures showing 7,000 British towns and villages.

FRANCIS FRITH'S LEGACY

Frith's legacy to us today is of immense significance and value, for the magnificent archive of evocative photographs he created provides a unique record of change in the cities, towns and villages throughout Britain over a century and more. Frith and his fellow studio photographers revisited locations many times down the years to update their views, compiling for us an enthralling and colourful pageant of British life and character.

We are fortunate that Frith was dedicated to recording the minutiae of everyday life, for it is this sheer wealth of visual data, the painstaking chronicle of changes in dress, transport, street layouts, buildings, housing, engineering and landscape that captivates us so much today. His remarkable images offer us a powerful link with the past and with the lives of our ancestors.

THE VALUE OF THE ARCHIVE TODAY

Computers have now made it possible for Frith's many thousands of images to be accessed almost instantly. Frith's images are increasingly used as visual resources, by social historians, by researchers into genealogy and ancestry, by architects and town planners, and by teachers involved in local history projects.

In addition, the archive offers every one of us an opportunity to examine the places where we and our families have lived and worked down the years. Highly successful in Frith's own era, the archive is now, a century and more on, entering a new phase of popularity. Historians consider the Francis Frith Collection to be of prime national importance. It is the only archive of its kind remaining in private ownership. Francis Frith's archive is now housed in an historic timber barn in the beautiful village of Teffont in Wiltshire. Its founder would not recognize the archive office as it is today. In place of the many thousands of dusty boxes containing glass plate negatives and an all-pervading odour of photographic chemicals, there are now ranks of computer screens. He would be amazed to watch his images travelling round the world at unimaginable speeds through internet lines.

The archive's future is both bright and exciting. Francis Frith, with his unshakeable belief in making photographs available to the greatest number of people, would undoubtedly approve of what is being done today with his lifetime's work. His photographs depicting our shared past are now bringing pleasure and enlightenment to millions around the world a century and more after his death.

AROUND PENARTH
AN INTRODUCTION

THE RENOWNED educationalist Jean Piaget once claimed that a childhood memory of an experience, person or place could be so strong that it might subconsciously dominate an adult's perception of a 'familiar something' for the rest of his or her life, long after those times seemed forgotten. This theory is certainly borne out by my recollection of long hot summer days in Penarth as a child in the early 1970s. These recollections have shaped my view of the town ever since, and it is they that I wish to share.

It is the memory of the journey that perhaps remains most vivid all these years on. Travelling the long straight length of Penarth Road, the busy conduit linking my hometown and our destination, anticipation would crackle and slowly build for the young backseat passengers. Hurried glances sought landmarks and familiar features en route. How close are we? What time will we arrive? I was usually first to spot it. To our right rose the huge plastic cigar, bizarrely illuminated at night, surmounting the façade of

THE PIER *c1955* P24145

the cigar factory. That was our touchstone, our marker. From this point on Cardiff was gone, and a special day in Penarth lay ahead.

Past the old Penarth Dock railway station, closed for business now but still clinging on to life along the town's twilight fringe. Past the grimy fronts of those Cogan houses unfortunate enough to be sited too close to the busy road and under the bridge. 'It's Brains You Want!' it proclaimed. We did and we had. This painted slogan of Cardiff's Brains Brewery was like a mantra to local drinkers, a rallying cry for it's devotees. We were all too aware of where the excitement of the seaside could be found. The neat colourful houses of Hill Terrace were perched like nesting birds on an arctic cliff. Surely their imperious position would provide a view of the sea through the vernal wilderness opposite? Whether they did or not I was certainly envious that they might.

Moving quickly through town, the attractions of the main drag, Windsor Road, would be half seen but fully appreciated. Glimmering like jewels were toyshops, sweets and newsagents piled high with the latest comics. On any other day (or in any other place) these sights would have encouraged a backseat clamour powerful enough to stop any family outing in its tracks. But not now – today we were going 'down the front' and nothing else mattered. Our destination was tantalisingly close. Encountering the roundabout at the Stanwell Road junction, it is difficult for us today to comprehend its absolute novelty when first constructed. It was met with curiosity and incredulity in equal measure; locals would pack the pavements in front of the banks just to observe what little traffic there was attempt to negotiate it. Lord Windsor and his spiritual heirs sitting on the council would have been proud. This was a dignified attraction in itself; no need for the tawdry delights and lurid thrills of nearby Barry Island – a rival to Penarth in geographic terms only. No need for Barry Island's roller coaster either. As Windsor Terrace gives way to Beach Road and the solid villas overlooking Alexandra Park, we have the drop. Oh, the drop! It would take my breath away and cause my stomach to somersault. We were cruising at altitude in our Mk 1 Cortina spacecraft, and my memories are golden - yet tarnished with my uncle, our driver, always taking that fiercely steep incline at a reckless un-safety belted speed. Hurtling past the overgrown 'secret' gates of the impressive Beach Road residences, all things left and right were a blur, but ahead was the sea – a vista unparalleled. Then as now, I cannot imagine a more dramatic approach to a British seaside resort or a headier introduction to its charms.

Once arrived, finding a parking space along the Esplanade on a summer's day could prove extremely difficult. The worsening problem had almost entered into local folklore, and for decades local traders had implored the council to rectify the situation, fearing loss of custom to the nearby beaches of Swanbridge, Lavernock or worse still the town's dual nemesis of Barry and Porthcawl. Where once from their Marine Parade homes the fabulously wealthy shipping magnates viewed the traffic (their own maritime traffic, that is) sailing in and out of Cardiff docks, any interested party with a telescope c1972 would have to be content monitoring a road traffic jam. A car park had long been established near Cliff

Hill, and the grounds of The Kymin, former home of John 'Friend of Freedom' Bachelor, narrowly escaped the same fate. Sadly, somewhat forgotten now, Bachelor's radical Liberalism had been the bane of the Tory dominated political scene in Cardiff. Such was the vitriol of the attack published in the Bute controlled 'Western Mail' on his death in 1883 that a bitter court case would ensue. Its final outcome was that the dead could not be libelled - a landmark ruling in English and Welsh law. Back in the 20th century the solution was to be perhaps the most reviled building in Penarth - and, I'm ashamed to admit, in some ways at the time my favourite.

Although two venerable reminders of the pre-developed seafront, Rock Villa and Balcony Villa, had given way to the Windsor Court in 1965, and the Sea Bank block of flats was raised at the foot of Beach Hill at much the same time, true venom was to be directed at the concrete multi-storey car park constructed on the furthest reach of the Esplanade towards Penarth Head. Its brutalist architecture and stylistic incongruity met with local outrage from the start, and one can only imagine the Council's arguments and agonies over its implementation. In late 1969 Glamorgan County Council finally approved Penarth Urban District Council's further plans to develop a leisure centre on one floor of the building. For many it would symbolise the antithesis of what the resort should be about, but for this young boy the magical room full of coca cola, pinball, dodgems and shooting games was to be a temporary (all-weather) paradise. I am sure that on quiet evenings if one tried really hard the sound of Lord Windsor turning in his grave was audible.

As the principal landowner in the area, he, alongside his trusted estate manager Robert Forrest and his architect Henry Snell, had from the early 1880s on set about transforming a drab fishing village (whose only recent incomers had been predominantly humble dock workers) into a prosperous town; it was to be both a destination and retreat for the extremely wealthy and an elegant and highly fashionable resort. The Countess of Plymouth herself was to be instrumental in this plan to create 'not only a place of great commercial activity, but to transform it into a beautiful and commodious watering place, a successful competitor with other places of summer resort, and one that will doubtless be very largely patronised by seaside visitors and summer excursionists'. This they managed with great aplomb, eschewing all kinds of vulgar entertainment and attraction, all the while following a self-imposed code of tact and restraint which soon became for the local press at least a byword for a peculiarly 'Penarthian' attitude as to what was deemed fit and proper for 'the finest seaside resort in Wales'. In modern parlance, through their determined vision and endeavours, Penarth had repositioned itself in the market by an energetic and consolidated move upwards. Woe betide those who had the temerity to bring their own refreshments onto the beach or offend the local populace with displays of lines of drying bathing costumes across the sandy stretches, then much more plentiful than now.

Hungry and thirsty visitors to the front had long been well served by local traders with Govier's Restaurant and the Gwalia Café occupying premises in Fredrick Speed's block of shops completed near the centre of the

Esplanade in 1904. This is to say nothing of the great popularity of the Esplanade Hotel, whose ground floor facilities were open to the public. By the time of your author's first visits, the celebrated Rabaiotti family managed no fewer than three food establishments along the Esplanade, with a fourth, an ice cream parlour on the pier, locked in mortal combat with a neighbouring Thayer's ice cream outlet. It is interesting that the pier at this time could also boast an antiques shop – pretty much unnoticed by myself at the time, but now, on reflection, a seemingly rather incongruous cuckoo in the retail nest.

But not all days in Penarth were ice creamed and sun drenched. Sometimes, whilst standing on the pier on rainy windswept early Sunday mornings, my uncle would valiantly attempt to keep me amused – my interest in the ongoing angling contests virtually nonexistent. Having been primed by my tattered 'Ladybird Book of Pirates', I found his tales of wreckers and wrongdoing along the beaches here enthralling.

Could the now tranquil Sully Island really have been the home of De Marisco, the notorious pirate dubbed the 'Night Hawk of the Bristol Channel'? It was said that of all the smugglers and buccaneers plying their nefarious trade along this coastline and hiding out in local caves, De Marisco was by far the most feared for his ruthlessness. Believed to be a mercenary knight arriving in South Wales with the Normans, his treachery would eventually result in banishment by the king and the forfeiture of his lands. For years he successfully wreaked his revenge by way of acts of terror and brutality. He and his rag-tag group of army deserters were to get their comeuppance on 14 July 1242. Sighting an apparently defenceless vessel drifting towards Lundy, De Marisco and his men left their hideout and sailed within touching distance of their booty. It was a trap – the 'stricken' boat was fully manned and armed. A bloody struggle concluded with the deaths of most of the pirates and the capture of their leader. The tyrannical reign of the 'Night Hawk'

LAVERNOCK, *St Mary's Well Bay c1955* L279012

would end with his execution. A semblance of peace was to return to the area that was only intermittently disturbed.

Perhaps the Barbarians rugby side, annually holed up in their Esplanade Hotel hideout, were the heirs to this buccaneering tradition. Their carousing tempered by the Corinthian spirit, any bloodshed was thankfully confined to the field of play, and the only piracy was the stealing of points from the opposition by way of tactics and skill. The Barbarians' regular appearance in the town was, up unto the early 1970s, a time of good humour and festivity only ending with the ultimate closure of the hotel and the team upping anchors for Cardiff.

Were these days of my childhood really a golden era for the resort? In truth, probably not, but it would take a lot to persuade me otherwise. Perhaps for the best part of a century the seafront has striven in vain to match the memory of the spectacular success and popularity, hard-won but always stylishly earned, of the town's late Victorian and Edwardian heyday. Resting on past glories has never been Penarth's style, but grand plans have always been tempered by harsh economic realities. As far back as the mid 1850s an elaborate scheme to divert the Taff and enclose the whole of Penarth Bay had to be scaled down. One can only marvel at the aborted plans to create a rail link skirting Penarth Head carrying passengers from Cardiff along the Esplanade to the very end of the pier to board the pleasure cruisers. The handsome look of the pier today belies some very lean years, years in which there was little in the council pot for its upkeep. Incarnations as nightclub, dance hall and even cinema had long sought the tourist's shilling. Accidental damage and enforced years of wartime neglect took a heavy toll. Some had even called for the pier to be scrapped and the council to cut its losses. These heretical voices were soon silenced.

A very real crisis was finally averted in the 1980s when the Cardiff Bay Development Corporation funded repairs to the structure of the Esplanade – it had appeared to be on the verge of collapse. Contained in this action is the bitter irony of the resort's contemporary dilemma. Lord Windsor and his acolytes, with all their aspiration, foresight and not a little snobbery, could never have believed that a day would be reached in which their elegant resort would be in a desperate competition for custom with their near neighbour the vast grimy landscape of Cardiff docks reborn as the shiny new 'Bay'. The battle is far from being lost. The town of Penarth has long been ranked as one of the most desirable places to live in the whole of Wales; its identity has been successfully kept quite distinct from that of the neighbouring capital. As I write this in February 2005, a 6 million pound project is in negotiation to revitalise the appearance of the Esplanade in a bid to recapture the excitement and élan that some may say has faded in recent years. I for one wish it every success. Until then, I invite you to treat yourself to a thoroughly enjoyable dose of nostalgia by way of these fabulously evocative photographs of Penarth and its near neighbours. So come on in and take a dip. The water's lovely!

PENARTH

WINDSOR ROAD *1896* 38718

A fine illustration of the commercialisation of Windsor Road – but the buildings on the extreme left and right are apparently still residential. The earliest plans were to centre the business heart of the town on Glebe Street and develop into Arcot Street. Times changed, and the fine residences of this stretch of Windsor Road were to be co-opted into service, albeit with the addition of extended frontages.

THE LANSDOWNE HOTEL *1896* 38719

Perhaps one of the less celebrated architects of the new Penarth was Frederick Speed, prolific at the turn of the century. A fine example of his building work, the Lansdowne Hotel, is pictured here. Both the nearby British Legion building and the Royal Buildings are also his. The block near the centre of the Esplanade, completed by Speed in 1904, was of major benefit to visitors, providing both restaurant and accommodation facilities.

▶ THE ROUNDABOUT
c1940 P24134

The south side of Windsor Road lay undeveloped until c1880 with the construction of the block seen here beyond the roundabout. The London & Provincial Bank established itself c1883, relocating to a vacant school building on the corner of Stanwell Road c1886. It became Barclays (left) after bank amalgamation of 1919. Originally a mere sub-branch of Cardiff's Bute Street, the growing stature of the town is evidenced by the bank's gaining of both 'full' status (c1886) and Bute Street's erstwhile manager, Mr H W Rice!

◀ STANWELL ROAD
c1955 P24123

Two landmarks oppose one another on a busy route from the railway station. In the shade of Christchurch Congregational's intricate Gothic spire the purpose built public library (a 'Carnegie Building') opened in 1905 on land provided by Lord Windsor. To the left is the Washington Super Cinema section of a bold 1930s block which was also designed to accommodate flats, shops and garages.

PENARTH

▲ ALL SAINTS' CHURCH *1896* 38722
Conceived in a typically robust style by John Coates Carter, the Victoria Road church is seen here in the first decade of its existence. Established as a daughter church to Penarth's parish church, St Augustine's, it has led an unfortunate life. It was destroyed by fire in 1927, and then the rebuilt and enlarged church was again partially destroyed in 1941 by enemy action.

◄ ST AUGUSTINE'S CHURCH
c1874 7030

This building replaced a much smaller church on the same site. The construction of the new St Augustine's began in 1865; dedication by the Bishop of Llandaff followed the next year. It was designed by William Butterfield in the prevailing neo-Gothic style, and much of its cost was met by the wealthy Windsor family. With its tower 300ft above sea level, it is probably the town's only building clearly recognisable from neighbouring Cardiff.

FRANCIS FRITH'S - AROUND PENARTH

ST AUGUSTINE'S CHURCH *1896* 38720

A wave of hostility met Butterfield's plans for the new church tower. This was an emotive issue, with the original long having been a landmark for locals and ships' pilots alike. The Admiralty, who themselves used the tower as a device on their charts, thought it prudent to intervene. Butterfield was forced to concede, building instead an even larger, more prominent version of the much loved original tower.

ALEXANDRA PARK
c1955 P24130

Taking its name from the wife of Edward VII, the park was officially opened on 25 June 1902 – the date scheduled (but not kept) for his coronation. The 1950s proved somewhat of a flat period for the park. 1951 witnessed the scrapping of its bandstand – a £62 repair estimate was deemed too costly, while 1956 saw the removal of its weather station. The park has long been famed for its topiary; a fine 'modern art' example stands far left.

THE WALK TO THE BEACH *1893* 32693
Such were the number of visitors navigating the overgrown and makeshift route from the town centre to the beach that the Windsor estate prioritised the construction of a more permanent path. A wide clearing was fashioned through the deeply wooded dell with two bridges traversing its streams, providing safe and unhindered passage.

PENARTH

THE DINGLE
1896 38730

Surrounded by some of the oldest trees in Penarth, children on the bridge gaze toward the camera. In 1884 gas lamps were installed along the route to the beach. Two years later the path was incorporated as a public highway with commensurate investment. The turn of the century would see the rustic bridges replaced by iron ones, asphalt laid in sections, and steps cut into the steepest slopes.

THE BEACH *1893* 32690

Although best known for its pebbled surface, low tide exposes a fair stretch of sand on Penarth Beach. Surrounded by groups of children intently digging, a gentleman in white (centre) appears to be holding an umbrella – a shelter from the noonday sun, or perhaps insurance against inclement weather? To the right, a small vessel festooned with flags is left scuppered by the retreat of the waves.

FRANCIS FRITH'S - AROUND PENARTH

PENARTH

THE BEACH
1893 32689

This is almost the same scene as in photograph 32690, page 23, but here we look eastwards. The two shots together provide an almost panoramic view of the coastline. Here the young boys explore the boat, whilst a lady appears only too aware of the photographer. This is the interim period of the seafront – most of the Esplanade had been in situ for a decade, but we are still one year away from the commencement of building the pier.

FRANCIS FRITH'S - AROUND PENARTH

PENARTH

THE CLIFFS
1893 32691

As we move further eastwards, the vista concludes with this dramatic portrayal of Penarth Head and its cliffs. From this low vantage point buildings on top of the headland go unseen, but the roof of Kymin House (left) peeps through the foliage. At the centre of the photograph a wooden slipway stands idle – this section of the beach is apparently deserted.

PENARTH

FROM THE PIER
1896 38465

The construction of the Esplanade c1883-84, costing in the region of £10,000, would provide a stable and stylish platform along which the town's chic new visitors could indulge in the fashion for promenading – seeing and being seen were of equal importance. No longer the clamber across rocks and amongst the throng. On such a feature, an esplanade linking all the seafront amenities, resorts were sold.

▼ THE ESPLANADE 1896 38728

Here the beautifully constructed Esplanade is viewed in close-up. Its creation was vital to form a refined loop around which the wealthy and fashionable could travel. Alighting at the railway station, it was now possible to travel comfortably by carriage down Beach Road, admire the Esplanade, and return up Cliff Hill back to your train via Marine Parade and Plymouth Road. This was a fantastic advertisement for an ambitious town.

► THE BOAT HOUSE AND THE BRIDGE 1896 38729

This fine building was built on the site of the relocated lifeboat station; its façade betrays its construction in stages. The initial phase was in 1884, followed by the next a year later in tandem with a change of name – the Boat Club becoming the Yacht Club. The third section was not completed until 1905. Behind the building, the iron bridge linking Windsor Gardens spans the old path to the coastguard's station.

PENARTH

◄ **THE BEACH**
1896 38462

A busy scene rich in period detail. In the foreground people access the beach via a slipway. In the distance a crowd gather to be entertained – could it be minstrels or a Punch and Judy show? A little closer, a group of donkeys await their rides. How ironic that only a decade earlier the resort had been disparagingly referred to as 'Donkey Island' – a withering appraisal of its coarse visitors and plebeian attractions.

► **THE PIER**
1896 38466

Wheeled bathing machines at the water's edge preserve the modesty of Victorian swimmers so none can be seen braving the waters. The vast majority of pleasure seekers here are not only on land but formally dressed. Those taking to the sea do so in rowing boats. The popularity of these inexpensive vessels for hire probably reached their zenith at the turn of the century.

FRANCIS FRITH'S - AROUND PENARTH

PENARTH

THE PIER
1896 38723

The clamour for a pier was such that even a second-hand one had been considered. An outraged public were relieved to witness work on a new pier by Mayoh's of Manchester in April 1894 and its subsequent opening the following year. With its florist (in the kiosk on the left) and tearoom (right), its pleasures were staid, but it would prove a considerable draw. Moreover it would be a perfect port of call for pleasure cruisers working the Channel.

PENARTH

THE PIER
1896 38464

With a beautifully attired young lady at its centre, this photograph brilliantly captures the fin de siecle elegance of the seafront. With acute business acumen, Penarth had rapidly established itself as possibly the most fashionable resort in Wales – bracketing itself with the likes of Brighton rather than with the brash vulgarity of Barry Island. Its long glorious summer seasons would only truly fade at the onset of war.

THE PIER
1896 38461

For many years hoards of revellers would descend on the beach from Cardiff via cheap ferry trips. By the 1870s, Robert Forrest knew that he could not stop the 'rabble' and their use of the beach, which he deemed 'not legitimate'. He did realise, however, that upgrading the facilities would attract a better class of visitor – cultured, refined but above all wealthy and willing to spend freely.

THE ESPLANADE HOTEL
From the Pier 1896 38727

Two important new buildings stand on the Esplanade. At the centre are the public swimming baths housing two saltwater pools, the larger capable of hosting international water polo matches and, when boarded over, doubling as gymnasium. Next door is the Esplanade Hotel, which from its inception proved an extremely popular watering hole that would soon become the spiritual home of the Barbarians rugby side. Note the intricate ironwork of the pier railings (extreme left).

▲ **WINDSOR GARDENS** *1893* 32687

By the close of the century, the town had attracted many of the wealthiest industrialists and shipping magnates intent on escaping an overcrowded Cardiff. The residences seen (right) through the shrubbery are their enclave – the grand villas of Bridgman Road and neighbouring Marine Parade. Not for them the common entrance to these gardens - special gates provided most exclusive access. The cannon to the left is a Boer War souvenir.

◀ **WINDSOR GARDENS** *1896* 38725

The laying out of Windsor Gardens in 1880 was an early manifestation of the 'new' Penarth, an integral part of the work to gentrify the seafront area. Like much of this remodelling, the plans for this 'dignified ribbon of land' were undertaken by Lord Windsor's St Fagans Estate manager, Robert Forrest, in conjunction with his architect Henry Snell.

▼ THE VIEW FROM WINDSOR GARDENS *1896* 38726

Here we have a glimpse of the pier through the 'fresh and luxuriant foliage' of the gardens. By this date the area had expanded southwards, no longer impeded by the dingle, with a bridge facilitating an extension of the parkland towards Cliff Road. With their magnificent sea view, away from the hustle and bustle of the beach, these gardens were quite literally a cut above.

► THE BAY
c1955 P24142

This striking view across the bay was taken from the grounds of The Kymin. The house is one of the very few left that are 'pre Esplanade', itself occupying the site of an earlier farm. Since its grounds were bisected by the redevelopment of Beach Road, the council initiated plans to purchase it in 1947. Original ideas to use its space for car parking were scrapped, and the house struggled to find a fitting use.

PENARTH

◀ **THE ESPLANADE**
c1955 P24146

With the council's eventual acquisition of the pier in 1924 their financial commitment to it and to the development of the Esplanade would be huge, and spread over decades of work. Years of inertia and neglect needed remedy: a new pavilion was built, and further development of Beach Road was undertaken to provide improved access to the front. This was to be a major investment of public money – the council gambled on the successful revival of the resort's fortunes.

▶ **THE PIER**
c1955 P24156

Just two years after the new pavilion's opening, a disaster was averted when bravery and decisive action prevented a blaze reaching it. During a dance on the August Bank Holiday of 1931 the old wooden Bijou Pavilion at the pier's seaward end was completely destroyed by fire. Boats were quickly mobilised to evacuate people from the damaged area, and we may be thankful that fatalities were avoided.

FRANCIS FRITH'S - AROUND PENARTH

PENARTH

THE BEACH AND THE ESPLANADE
c1955 P24155

Those seeking refreshment in 1955 were certainly well catered for. Excluding the Esplanade Hotel, no fewer than five cafes operated along the front, including Forte's splendid ice cream parlour. A further two confectioners and a snack bar could be found on the pier. Accommodation was also plentiful. Although increasingly a magnet for day-trippers, by the end of the decade the town boasted two hotels, and four large and up to seventy-five smaller guesthouses.

PENARTH

THE BEACH
1955 P24151

Beyond the headland, the intrusion of industrial Cardiff into this view illustrates just how close the large docks were – albeit as the crow flies. This northern beach area had, with grim humour, been christened 'The Dardanelles' on account of this particular section of coastline's heavy fortification during the dark days of the war. Searchlights, once mounted on the pier, stood rusting here for many years.

FRANCIS FRITH'S - AROUND PENARTH

PENARTH

THE PIER
c1955 P24144

The 600-capacity New Pavilion opened in May 1929 with attendant shops, tea lounges and terrace. It was built by E J Smith of Cardiff in a vaguely eastern Art Deco style, and the building material was (the then) ultra modern ferro-concrete. Many mourned the loss of the pointed roof frontage of the old café and shops, but a link with the past was maintained by the redeployment of the original main gate as a side entrance (left, behind the van). By the time of this photograph, the Pavilion had metamorphosed into the Marina Ballroom, having spent a short period as a cinema.

PENARTH

THE PIER
c1955 P24157

Penarth's post-war attempts to re-establish itself as a first-class resort were to be dealt a serious blow in May 1947. The huge Canadian vessel 'Port Royal Park', driven broadside into the pier during a gale, inflicted structural damage so severe that demolition was considered. That scenario was dismissed, but costs to underpin the pier were to total £28,000, and further revenue was lost by the absence of steamer custom during the period of repair.

FRANCIS FRITH'S - AROUND PENARTH

PENARTH

THE PIER
c1955 P24145

The 1950s were to be relatively happy years for the resort - a brief renaissance was enjoyed. But its traditional role was drawing to a close. Campbell's ships still visited, and although their operations were drastically scaled down, the end of the summer season was still a time for fireworks, parties and celebration. Evenings saw the pier, the Esplanade and the Italian Gardens festooned with lights – restrictions were finally lifted in 1949.

▶ **THE ITALIAN GARDENS**
c1940 P24138

Perhaps more redolent of the English Riviera than the Continent, the terraced gardens facing the ocean, opened in 1926, were to be an instantaneous and roaring success. The impetus for their creation lay with Ursula Thompson (a Kew-trained gardener) and her association with the chairman of the council, Constance Maillard. Their enthusiasm for such a project prompted the council to develop the previously inadequately used open space.

◀ **THE PIER AND THE ITALIAN GARDENS**
c1940 P24131

The name 'Italian Gardens' eventually stuck – a handful of others were also applied in the early years. Much of the job of excavating the site had been accomplished by hand, an arduous task necessitated by the close confines of the work and its steep backdrop. The original iron railings seen here skirting the lowest terrace were removed during the Second World War – chains eventually replaced them in 1948.

PENARTH

▲ **A PLEASURE STEAMER LEAVING THE PIER** *c1955* P24148

Pictured here in really what was the twilight of its golden age, the pier had long been the point of embarkation for daytrips to destinations along the Bristol Channel. With the introduction of the original 'Waverley' vessel in 1888, and boasting a 13-strong fleet by 1914, the 'White Funnels' of P A Campbell & Co were to establish their dominance in cross-channel travel.

◄ **THE ESPLANADE**
From Windsor Gardens c1955 P24152

The introduction of 'No Parking' markings along parts of the Esplanade was inevitable. The trend for day tripping and the increase in car ownership were to prove a bane for the council. Provision for parking was woefully inadequate – the construction of the controversial multi-storey car park was some way off. The purchase c1952 of the Cliff Green site adjacent to Cliff Walk would temporarily alleviate the problem.

FRANCIS FRITH'S - AROUND PENARTH

PENARTH

THE HOVERCRAFT
1963 P24184

In a bid to recapture the public's imagination and recreate the excitement and glamour of cross-channel travel, Campbell's were to introduce a hovercraft service in the summer of 1963. The journey between Penarth and Weston-super-Mare could be accomplished in just 12 minutes. Never financially viable, the experimental service, its novelty not withstanding, was discontinued at the end of the season.

PENARTH

THE BEACH AND THE ESPLANADE
c1960 P24194

With the last significant addition to the Esplanade being the Italian Gardens of the 1920s, only the cars (far right) betray this photograph's modernity. However, the landscape of the Esplanade was on the verge of a dramatic and highly controversial change. In November 1959 the council gave support for a 'skyscraper block of Continental styled luxury flats' at the bottom of Beach Hill – a 10-storey block heralded as 'the most modern in the country', comparable only with a similar development in Zurich. With this, and plans for a seafront multi-storey complex, in Penarth the modern architectural genie was well and truly out of the bottle.

PENARTH FROM THE AIR

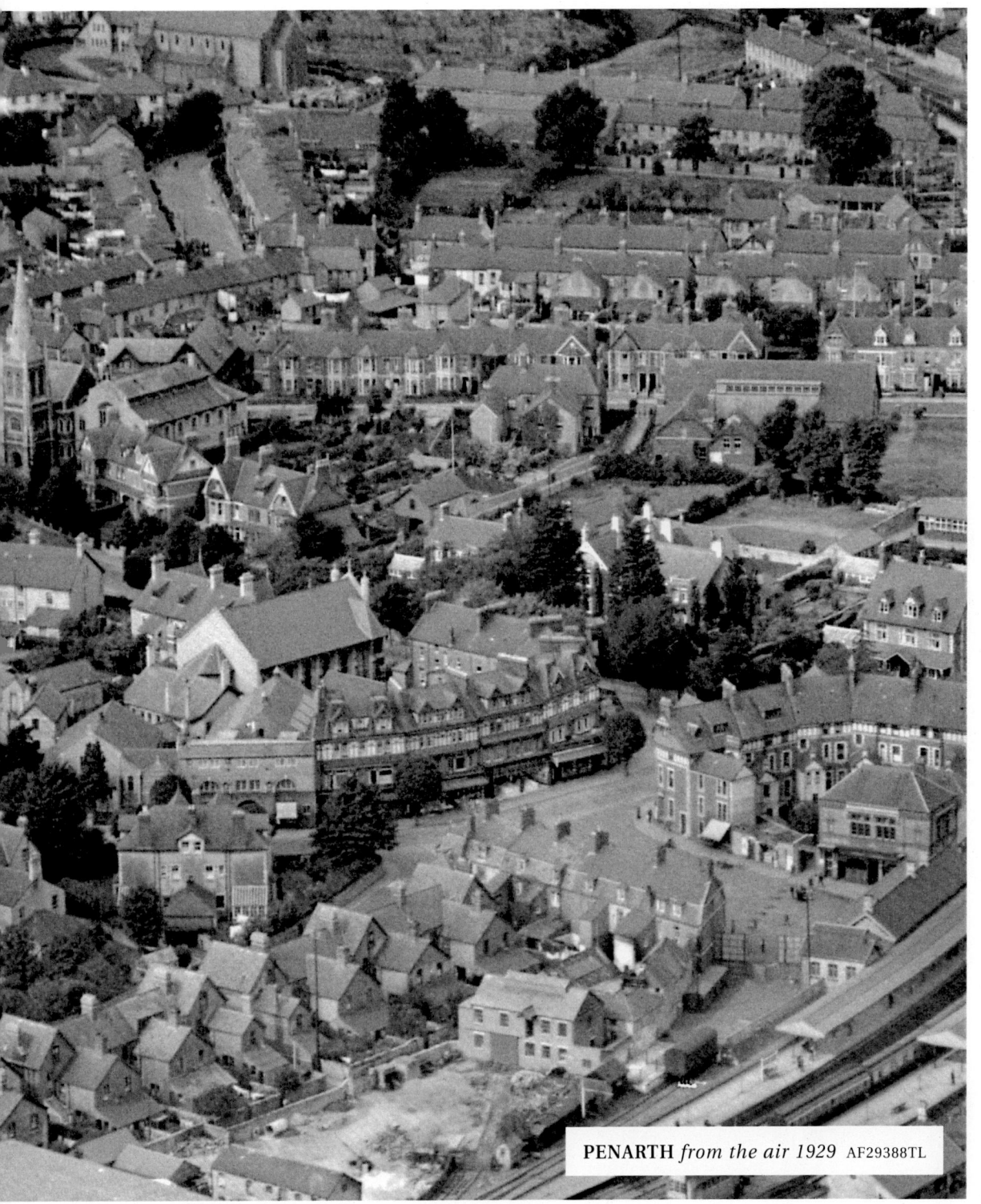

PENARTH *from the air 1929* AF29388TL

LLANDOUGH AND SULLY

LLANDOUGH
St Dochdwy's Church
c1955 L280002

Although the church is of relatively modern construction – it was built in the mid 1860s - the site has religious significance probably dating back to before the Norman Conquest. At first glance the church's most striking feature appears to be the contrasting steep and shallow pitched roofs; but a closer look identifies the ancient stone column of an Ibric cross (furthest in second row of graves from left), indicative of early Welsh Christianity in the area.

LLANDOUGH AND SULLY

LLANDOUGH
The Hospital, the Nurses' Home c1955 L280005

Executed in an imposing neo Georgian style, the hospital opened in 1933 and was completed the following year. Declining to adapt Edward Seward's original plans, the replacement architects, Willmott & Smith, drew up new ones at their own expense. The building was almost universally lauded for its modernity, and no major additions to the site were undertaken until the mid 1960s. The hospital's inaugural year was not without controversy – a minor furore ensued after an 'important post' was awarded to a sister of a city councillor.

LLANDOUGH, *The Hospital, the Main Entrance c1955* L280008

The hospital's 'attractive appearance belies ... its age'. So proclaimed the South Wales Echo in its December 1956 review of the facility. At this time, Wales's most modern teaching hospital could boast 379 beds, with an aim to reach the 1000 mark. Reporters enthused over the retention of the hospital's rural aspect and warm, sunny wards, even judging its kitchens 'the finest in the country'.

LLANDOUGH, *The Merry Harrier c1955* L280006
This is the second incarnation of the pub – the original was destroyed by fire in 1907. With the advent of a regular bus service in the 1920s, this popular local became a favourite stopping-off point between Cardiff and Barry. The 'harrier' of its name refers to a foxhound-like dog especially bred for hunting rabbits – a historical reminder of the sporting pursuits of the local agricultural workers.

LLANDOUGH AND SULLY

SULLY
St John the Baptist's Church and the Lychgate c1950 S437006

The church dates back to the Norman Conquest, but very little of the original church remains; the initial period of restoration in the 1820s dramatically altered its structure. Local people believe that the yew tree near the path was planted in the early 19th century to deter the playing of ball games. A striking 20th-century addition is the lychgate – a commemoration of the end of the First World War.

SULLY, *The Hospital, the Nurses' Home c1950* S437001

On land acquired from Hayes Farm, the architects W A Pite, Son & Fairweather constructed Sully Hospital between 1932 and 1936 to a competition-winning design. For many years the facility operated as one of the primary treatment centres for tuberculosis in Britain. Created in the International Art Deco style, its north facing entrance (pictured here) housed the nurses' quarters.

LLANDOUGH AND SULLY

SULLY
The Hospital c1950
S437002

Ideally located to take advantage of the beneficial properties of sea air, the south-facing hospital wards further benefited from the shelter of existing trees. With its highly stylised stair towers and full-length windows, the hospital would eventually be recognised as one of the most outstanding 20th-century buildings in Wales. How sad it is that a Grade II listing could not prevent its pitiful decline and period of disuse.

FRANCIS FRITH'S - AROUND PENARTH

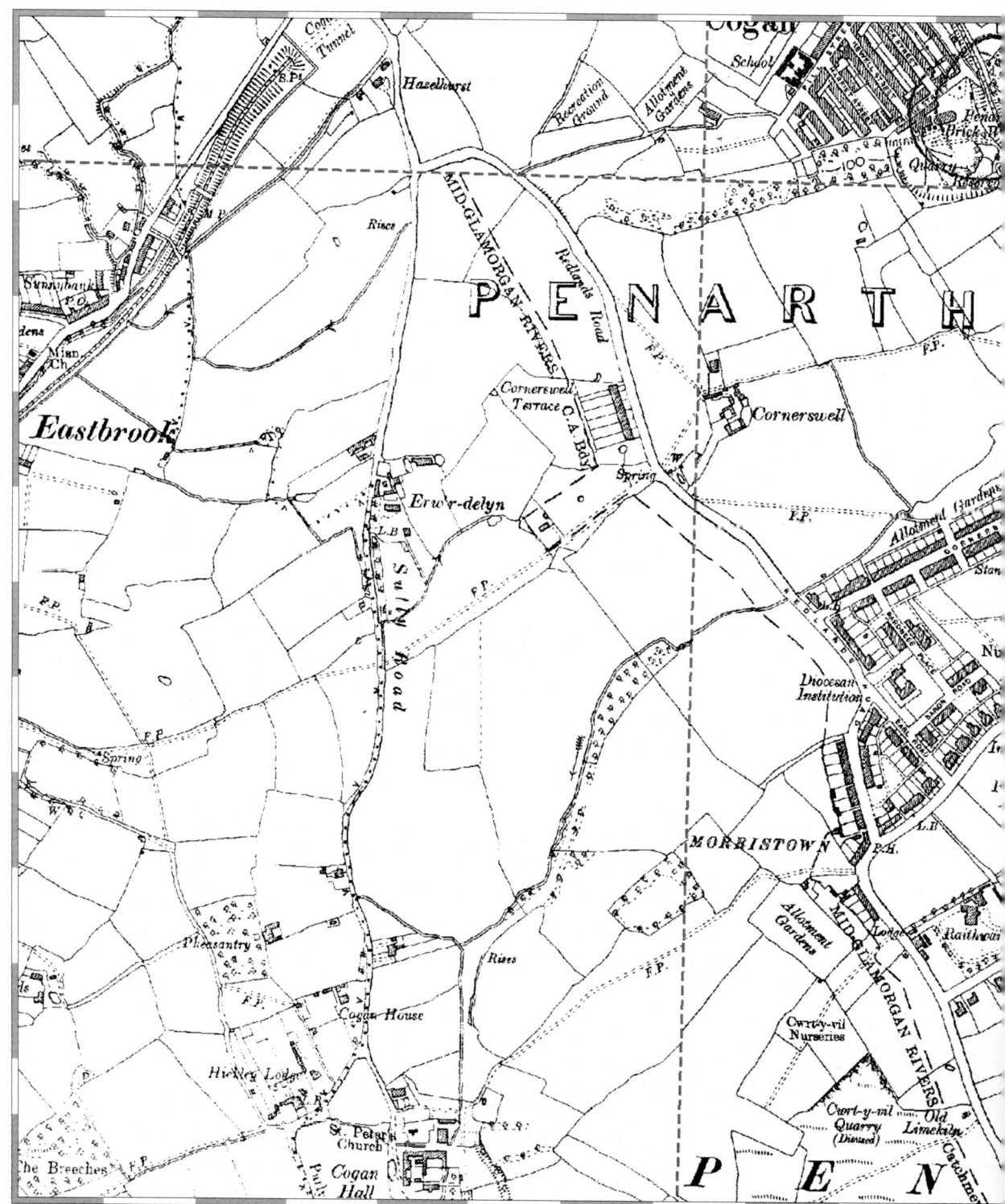

ORDNANCE SURVEY MAP OF PENARTH AND SURROUNDING AREAS c1900

FRANCIS FRITH'S - AROUND PENARTH

LAVERNOCK AND SWANBRIDGE

LAVERNOCK, *St Mary's Well Bay c1955* L279005
Long before the advent of mass tourism, the coastline here had been exploited as a source of income for local people. During the 18th and 19th centuries many buildings (including the old railway station) were constructed with rock quarried from the beach. Much of the material was hauled to the water's edge for transportation by boat. Shipments of stone to Cardiff helped satisfy demand for paving stones in the rapidly expanding town.

LAVERNOCK AND SWANBRIDGE

LAVERNOCK
St Mary's Well Bay c1955
L279012

Beyond the happy holidaymakers the distinctively striped rock face, vividly illustrated here, is a signature feature of the cliff face between Barry and Penarth. Beauty, however, comes at a price. As far back as 1977 measures to combat coastal erosion around the bay were estimated to cost £170 000. More recently, in October 2004, the Environment Agency rejected plans for luxury apartments overlooking St Mary's Well Bay for fear of flooding.

LAVERNOCK, *The Caravan Site c1955* L279017
Holidaymakers at this time could be forgiven for thinking that there was something of an army camp about the site! In addition to some of the chalets having originally been used as barracks, the continued existence of abandoned gun emplacements, storage lockers and searchlights were reminders of how heavily defended this stretch of coastline was – it had been vital to protect the Severn Estuary and the ports of Cardiff and Barry.

LAVERNOCK AND SWANBRIDGE

LAVERNOCK
St Mary's Well Bay
c1965 L279139

'Quick Mum, get the ice cream whilst there's no queue!' The much loved and heavily patronised refreshment kiosk was an obligatory port of call for all families enjoying a day out at the beach. Stories of the length of time spent standing in line at the height of the season have become part of local legend, but it was always worth the wait. A 'Wall's Sunspot' indeed!

LAVERNOCK
St Mary's Well Bay
c1965 L279140

Within view of their parents' caravans groups of children could play unsupervised. With Camp Wardens on hand to curtail anything too boisterous, this now seems a golden era – carefree youngsters left to their own devices. After exploring the beach all day, they were guaranteed to re-appear at the caravan door at teatime. What current Health & Safety legislation would make of the roped climbing frame and the trampoline, however, is debateable.

SWANBRIDGE
The Manor House and Spinney Holiday Park c1955 S438030

The Spinney, as the manor house of the parish of Sully, was sold at auction in 1938 as part of 164 acres of land that included Sully Island. The Spinney was already a tourist facility, for the sale included the tea lawn, the refreshment kiosk and a car park. A less tangible asset would be the entitlement of the buyer to the 'reputed Lordship of the Manor of Sully'.

LAVERNOCK AND SWANBRIDGE

▲ **SWANBRIDGE,** *The Spinney Holiday Camp c1955* S438009

A grand residence gives way to accommodation somewhat more compact and bijou. The interior of The Spinney was particularly handsome, with dark oak and mahogany fixtures throughout. Although relatively modern, the house incorporated both a 17th-century fireplace and panelling reputedly salvaged from an ancient Bristol church. The terraced gardens were its equal – both tropical and alpine collections shared space with an orchard and beautifully maintained tennis courts.

◄ **SWANBRIDGE**
The Beach c1955
S438010

Bathers beware! In the late 1950s, prompted by the highly visible contamination of the coastline, scientists undertook an extensive survey of the problem. The area was a victim of the remarkable tidal flow of the Severn, which caused a horrific amount of raw sewage to float back to shore. Shocked by its findings, the 1964 report described the situation as 'a salutary reflection on our sense of values as a civilised community'.

◀ **SWANBRIDGE**
The Spinney c1955
S438048

Situated to the right, beyond the low white building (later to become the Captain's Wife public house) is Sully Island. It is accessible by foot at low tide, and many a holidaymaker has fallen foul of the tide's rapid reversal – a sobering cold night spent on the island their reward. It is difficult to believe that the Town Planning scheme once scheduled portions of the island for development at a rate of 12 houses per acre.

LAVERNOCK AND SWANBRIDGE

◀ **SWANBRIDGE**
*The Spinney
Caravan Park
c1955* S438034

Swanbridge and Sully Island, once the haunt of wreckers and pirates, would play host to an equally enthusiastic yet more peaceful group of invaders each summer! The post-war period saw a boom in British caravanning - 'cheap' continental package tours were still beyond the reach of most working people. The stunning coastline here, easily accessible from the B4267, was a considerable draw.

◀ **SWANBRIDGE**
The Slipway c1950
S438307

Even at this time, the visual appearance of the slipway at Swanbridge had become a cause for concern. The slipway was privately owned, but with perhaps too little investment the reinforced concrete sections had begun to deteriorate and break up, with the metal rods exposed and rusting. It is sad fact that this situation has never been adequately rectified.

PENARTH FROM THE AIR

PENARTH *from the air 1929* AF29388TR

FRANCIS FRITH'S - AROUND PENARTH

DINAS POWIS

DINAS POWIS
St Andrew's Major Church c1955 D31030

Typical of so many Glamorgan churches, St Andrew's traces its roots back to the Norman occupation – its nave and chancel are believed to date from the 13th century. Though the church was much altered during the 1900s, a significant addition was undertaken in 1921. A long-blocked-up archway was reopened and its connecting chapel rebuilt in memory of the Lord of the Manor, General Lee, who had been a highly respected and 'generous patron' of the village church.

DINAS POWIS
Cwrt-y-Ala 1900 45553

Demolished in 1939, this house is thought to be the third dwelling on the site – the first was possibly a Norman tower. A short-lived second villa gave way to the house pictured here, built by Edward Haycock c1820. Occupied by the Rous and later Brain families, much of what we view here beyond the artificial lakes is the architectural additions of c1850-60.

DINAS POWIS, *The Common c1965* D31080

The relative tranquillity of this scene belies the common's historic role as a venue for altogether more rowdy activities. Extremely popular in the Vale were 'Gwylmabsant' – days of celebration and revelry of ecclesiastic origin. By the 18th century these boisterous gatherings had become distinctly non-secular and the scourge of Methodism. John Wesley himself bore witness to a 'revel' in Dinas Powis on 14 September 1741.

▶ DINAS POWIS
Highwalls Road c1960 D31037

Free from traffic and flanked by the old cottages, this post-war scene evokes an essence of earlier village days. The Twyn, the triangle of land on the right, so long the centre of the community, took shape in the late 1880s. This square, newly raised and planted with trees, was financed by the sale of part of the common to the Barry Docks & Railway Company – the shortfall was met by General Lee.

◀ DINAS POWIS
The Square c1960 D31031

The erection of the war memorial proved to be both protracted and controversial. Although a local committee had met in 1919 to discuss ideas for the project, building work would not begin until 16 years later! Even then, many villagers objected to the removal of trees to accommodate the structure. Alternative plans for a monument included a more elaborate cross design and the complete diversion of monies raised to fund a hospital instead.

DINAS POWIS

▲ **DINAS POWIS,** *The Square c1965* D31081

The early 1960s witnessed a significant increase in traffic through the area, in part due to the further increase in car ownership and commuting. The Twyn itself was threatened by Glamorgan County Council's plans for road widening – a project that would have resulted in the loss of a large section of the square. Local outrage scotched these plans, and the greened area remained intact minus only a nearby gas lamp.

◄ **DINAS POWIS** *Highwalls Avenue c1955* D31054

This view up Parish Road affords a glimpse of what was a centre of communication for the village. Brecon House (third from left) operated as a telegraphic office and later as the village telephone exchange until 1937 – a new automated system forced relocation. Next door, to its left, stands the Boy Scout hut that would be destroyed by fire in 1958.

▼ DINAS POWIS, Cardiff Road c1955 D31024

Major improvements in transport facilities around 1890 put the industries of Barry and Cardiff in easy reach for the first time. Dinas Powis would thus attract incomers in need of accommodation, and an extensive building plan would rapidly expand the boundaries of the town. Cardiff Road (pictured here) is a classic example of these new dwellings, with the finest houses executed by Dashwood Caple.

▶ DINAS POWIS
Mill Road c1960 D31039

A product of the increasing urbanisation of Dinas Powis at the close of the 19th century, Mill Road preserves the name of the nearby Mill Farm. On the horizon, beyond the similarly derived Mill Brook Road, stands the imposing Ardwyn. Our vantage point for this view is near to St Peter's Church, whose construction in the late 1920s made use of stone recycled from the defunct Cyfarthfa iron works.

DINAS POWIS
The Tennis Courts
c1955 D31026

Dinas Powis Tennis Club was founded in 1901, thanks to the generosity of General Lee as Lord of the Manor. Premises were amicably shared with the Bowls Club. The club expanded in 1954 with the shrewd acquisition of the neighbouring Bryneithen field. The following year, interest in this already popular facility soared owing to its inclusion in a series of BBC programmes based on South Wales clubs.

DINAS POWIS
The Bowling Green
c1955 D31028

Sited imperiously overlooking the bowling green is the fine Victorian residence Merevale; its foundation stone is dated 7 September 1893. The villa, demolished in August 1973, had been home to key figures in the community. One such occupant was Lillie Thomas, an honorary Commander of the Red Cross who did sterling work organising local facilities for the convalescence of the wounded home from the First World War.

FRANCIS FRITH'S - AROUND PENARTH

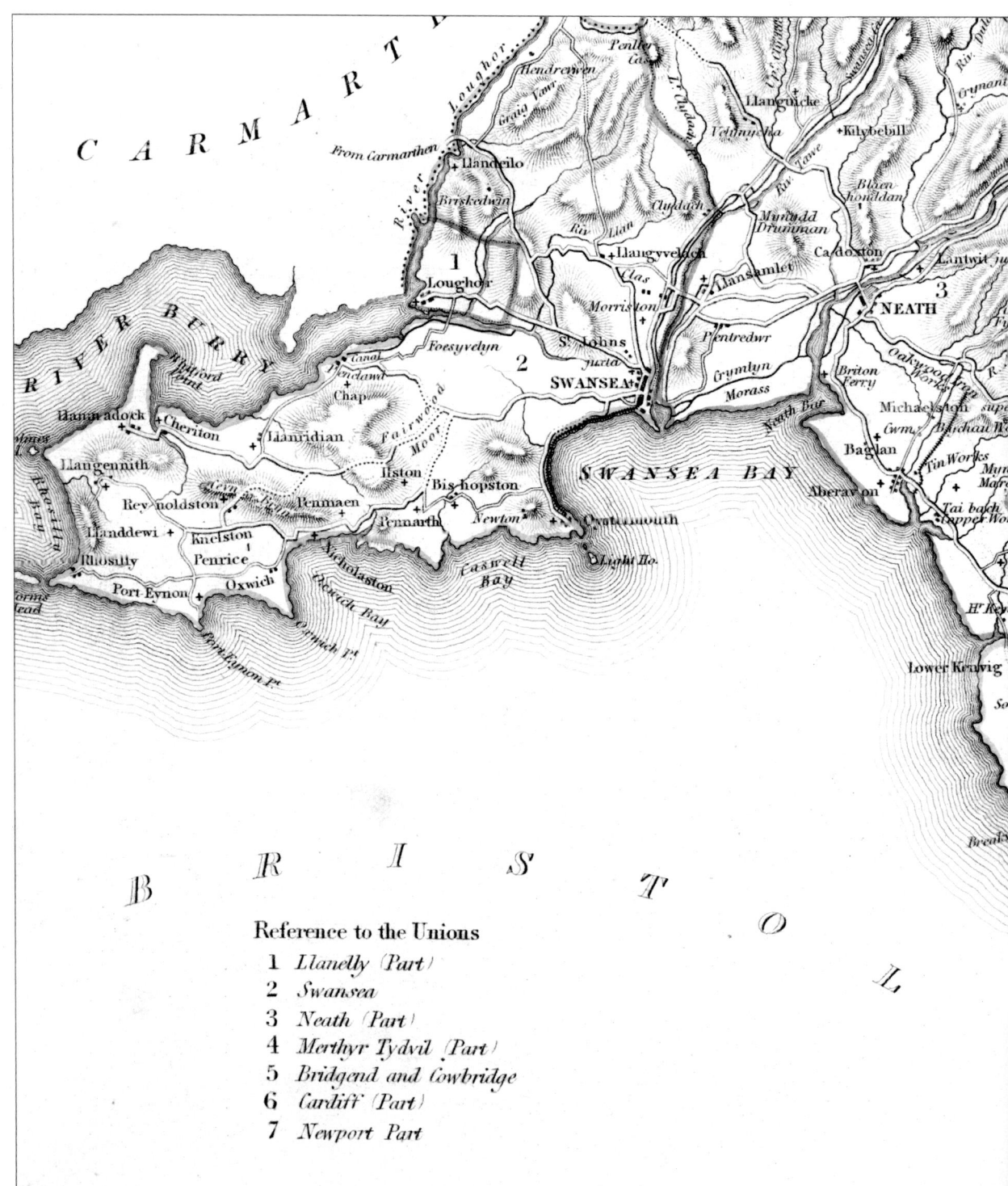

Reference to the Unions
1. Llanelly (Part)
2. Swansea
3. Neath (Part)
4. Merthyr Tydvil (Part)
5. Bridgend and Cowbridge
6. Cardiff (Part)
7. Newport Part

GLAMORGANSHIRE COUNTY MAP

GLAMORGANSHIRE COUNTY MAP *showing Penarth and surrounding areas c1850*

FRANCIS FRITH'S - AROUND PENARTH

ST FAGANS, ST NICHOLAS AND WENVOE

ST FAGANS
The Welsh Folk Museum Grounds c1960 S16010

Arguably more appropriately termed a mansion, the 'new' St Fagans Castle stands atop its impressive terraced gardens. The original castle, built in Norman times for the Le Sor family, fell into ruin early in its life to be replaced by a typically Elizabethan house. The 'Cambrian Traveller's Guide' of 1813 was a little sceptical, pointedly recording that 'the village contains a castle of somewhat modern construction'.

ST FAGANS
Welsh Folk Museum Formal Gardens c1960 S16007

Gifted by the Earl of Plymouth in 1947, the castle and its gardens were not only to become the centrepiece of the museum, but also an integral component. Used to exhibit the daily life of the Welsh gentry, they were, for the first three years of the museum's life, its very fine but sole attraction – the first reconstructed building in the grounds was not completed until 1951.

ST FAGANS, ST NICHOLAS AND WENVOE

ST NICHOLAS
The Village c1965
S436009

There is no general consensus as to the origin of 'St Nicholas' as a place name. Some believe that it is derived from the phosphorescent light effect seen around vessels in the nearby Bristol Channel, sometimes referred to by its Russian name 'St Nicholas's Lights'. At the time of this photograph the population of the parish had fallen to 326 – not until the 1980s would it match its 1950s high.

ST NICHOLAS, *The Village c1960* S436012
Seemingly indifferent to its position beside the busy thoroughfare connecting Cardiff and Cowbridge, Church Hall House (pictured) stands testament to a romanticised Victorian vision of a pre-industrial Britain. Built in 1898 in a William Morris-inspired Arts and Crafts style, the house boasts a distinctive stone, brick and render façade topped by terracotta tiles and an exaggerated turret.

ST NICHOLAS
The Green and the Memorial c1960
S436010

Initially commissioned to honour those of the parish who fell in the First World War, the simple Celtic cross of the war memorial was to be sadly amended in the aftermath of the Second World War with the loss of four local men. Corporal Cyril Channon died as a Japanese POW, Gunner Alec Collins was lost at sea with Captain John Duncan, and Lieutenant Rhys Thomas was killed in action.

WENVOE, *The Castle 1899* 43468

How sad – this is the end of our photographic journey around this part of the Vale of Glamorgan. Built for Peter Birt in the 1770s to a design by Robert Adam, this grand residence was for many years renowned for its beautiful interiors, their opulence virtually unparalleled in South Wales. From its pink and green dining room, a 19th-century visitor could wander throughout the castle enthralled by its vast and remarkable collection of stuffed animals on display.

INDEX

PENARTH
Alexandra Park 22
All Saints' Church 19
Bay 38
Beach 23, 24-25, 31, 40-41, 42-43, 54-55
Boat House 30
Cliffs 26-27
Dingle 23, 24-25
Esplanade 30, 38-39, 40-41, 51, 54-55
Esplanade Hotel 36
From the Pier 28-29
Hovercraft 52-53
Italian Gardens 50
Lansdowne Hotel 16-17
Pier 10, 31, 32-33, 34-35, 36, 39, 44-45, 46-47, 48-49, 50
Pleasure Steamer leaving the Pier 51
Roundabout 18
St Augustine's Church 19, 20-21
Stanwell Road 18
Walk to the Beach 22
Windsor Gardens 37, 38
Windsor Road 15

DINAS POWIS
St Andrew's Major Church 76

Bowling Green 81
Cardiff Road 80
The Common 77
Cwrt-y-Ala 77
Highwalls Road 78-79
Highwalls Avenue 79
Mill Road 80
The Square 78, 79
The Tennis Court 80-81

LAVERNOCK
The Caravan Site 67
St Mary's Well Bay 13, 66, 67, 68-69, 70-71

LLANDOUGH
St Dochdwy's Church 58
The Hospital, the Main Entrance 59
The Hospital, the Nurses' Home 59
The Merry Harrier 60

ST FAGANS
The Welsh Folk Museum Gardens 84
The Welsh Folk Museum Grounds 84

ST NICHOLAS
The Green and the Memorial 86-87
The Village 85

SULLY
St John the Baptist's Church and the Lychgate 61
The Hospital 62-63
The Hospital, the Nurses' Home 61

SWANBRIDGE
Beach 71
Holiday Park 70
Manor House and Spinney
Slipway 73
Spinney Caravan Park 72-73
Spinney Holiday Camp 71

WENVOE
The Castle 88

NAMES OF PRE-PUBLICATION BUYERS

THE FOLLOWING PEOPLE HAVE KINDLY SUPPORTED THIS BOOK BY SUBSCRIBING TO COPIES BEFORE PUBLICATION.

D M & C A Baker, Penarth
In memory of Kath & Bill Baker, Penarth
Blakeborough-Woodward, Penarth & Tervuren
Harold & Rhona Boudier, Stanwell Road
Glyn, Susan, Emily & Jamie Boulton, Penarth
Bradley's of 'The House'
Richard & Ruth Brennan, Dinas Powys
Sarah Broughton (nee Leyshon), Penarth
Henry J & Joan E Brown, Penarth
Mr T S & Mrs H P Brunker
John & Lenna Buck, Penarth
Cardiff & South Wales Advertiser
Geoffrey & Pauline Cheetham, Kensington, Xmas 2005
In memory of Edgar Clarke
Joan Collins
Mr James & Mrs Sally Coombs
Andrew Coslett, Penarth
Mr A N Couch & Mrs P M Couch
Thelma & Christopher Crawley
The Cullen Family of Llandough
Mike & Diane Davies, Llandough
Mr M W G & Mrs A Davies, Penarth
The Thomas Davies Family, Penarth
For our grandchild, Amaylia Peta Anna Dewis
Mr R T J Dyer & Mrs S M Dyer, Penarth
Michael Fellows, Cogan
Seimon, Carol, Dewi, Rhys Fford, Penarth
Brenda & Peter Fielding, Penarth
Gordon Fussell, Penarth
Robert Galley
Adrian George & Family, Penarth
Ian & Anita Gill (nee Churchill)

Roy & June Goddard, Penarth
Colin & Yvonne Grandin & Sam of Penarth
The Harrison Family
The Haven, Penarth
The Hewitt Family, Redlands Road
To Alan Hill on his birthday
Mr M Hill, Colwinston
Mr & Mrs J A Holder and daughters, Penarth
The Howells/Hooper Family, Penarth
To Pat Hubbard from a grateful neighbour
Melvin Hudd, Cogan
Maureen Irvine, Llantwit Major
The Jalil Family, Penarth
Mr E & Mrs S James, Penarth
The former Mayor of Penarth, Bill Jeffcott and his wife Min
The John & Midlane Family
Kim Johnson on your 50th, love Mum & Dad
Mr A J King, Penarth
Jason L Knott & Leona C Knott
Mr & Mrs W N E Ledbury, Penarth
Ken & Janice Lee, Penarth
Mr A D & Mrs A J McCulloch, Penarth
The McKinty Family, Penarth
To Craig Paul Marsh, Happy 22nd Birthday
The Mason Family, Penarth
June A Massey, Penarth, in loving memory of Albert & Emily Massey
The Massy Family, Norwich, Hadlow, Copt Hewick
The Mathieson Family, Penarth
Mr K J Morson & Mrs E A Morson
The Nurse Family of Cedar Way, Penarth
Mr C G Palmer & Mrs D I Palmer, Penarth

Frederick J Potter, Penarth

To Lorna Prance, Happy Birthday, love Mum

For my family and late parents, Moya Price, Penarth

G L Price, Penarth

The Pringle Family, Earl Road, Penarth

Jane & Alvin Rees, Sarasota, Florida, Xmas 2005

Ted, Edna & Meriyn Rees, Westbourne Road

In memory of the Rowland & Woolway Families, Penarth

Ben Salter

G Salter

The Samuel Family, Penarth

Richard, Liz, Isabel & Carys Stephens

Robert, Becky & Ruby Myfanwy Stephens

Brian & Avril Stephens, Robert & Richard

Margaret & Phil Stockwell, Penarth

Mr P W Stockwell, Penarth

To Zed, Holly & Megan Stong, love Mum

The Summers Family, Penarth

In memory of Les & Eileen Sweetland

In memory of Alan 'Yabow' Todd, Penarth

To Seren Vickers on her tenth birthday

The Wannell Family, Llandough

For Michael & Bernice Ward, our parents

In memory of Mrs Cecilia Watson, Penarth

Mr John D Wilce

To Robert, in memory of Dad, A G Williams

To Susan, in memory of Dad, A G Williams

To Terry, in memory of Dad, A G Williams

Rob Williams, Sully

To Kay Wisdom, Happy Birthday, love Mum

John Wreford, Penarth

Peggy & Pat Wright, Cambridge

FRITH PRODUCTS & SERVICES

Francis Frith would doubtless be pleased to know that the pioneering publishing venture he started in 1860 still continues today. Over a hundred and forty years later, The Francis Frith Collection continues in the same innovative tradition and is now one of the foremost publishers of vintage photographs in the world. Some of the current activities include:

INTERIOR DECORATION

Today Frith's photographs can be seen framed and as giant wall murals in thousands of pubs, restaurants, hotels, banks, retail stores and other public buildings throughout the country. In every case they enhance the unique local atmosphere of the places they depict and provide reminders of gentler days in an increasingly busy and frenetic world.

PRODUCT PROMOTIONS

Frith products are used by many major companies to promote the sales of their own products or to reinforce their own history and heritage. Frith promotions have been used by Hovis bread, Courage beers, Scots Porage Oats, Colman's mustard, Cadbury's foods, Mellow Birds coffee, Dunhill pipe tobacco, Guinness, and Bulmer's Cider.

GENEALOGY AND FAMILY HISTORY

As the interest in family history and roots grows world-wide, more and more people are turning to Frith's photographs of Great Britain for images of the towns, villages and streets where their ancestors lived; and, of course, photographs of the churches and chapels where their ancestors were christened, married and buried are an essential part of every genealogy tree and family album.

FRITH PRODUCTS

All Frith photographs are available Framed or just as Mounted Prints and unmounted versions. These may be ordered from the address below. Other products available are - Calendars, Jigsaws, Canvas Prints, Mugs, Tea Towels, Tableware and local and prestige books.

THE INTERNET

Over several hundred thousand Frith photographs can be viewed and purchased on the internet through the Frith websites!

For more detailed information on Frith products, look at **www.francisfrith.com**

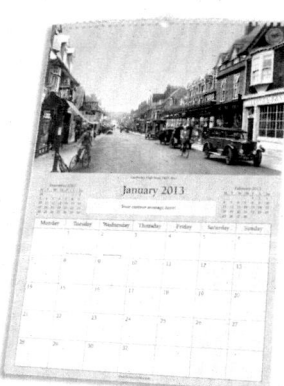

See the complete list of Frith Books at: www.francisfrith.com
This web site is regularly updated with the latest list of publications from The Francis Frith Collection. If you wish to buy books relating to another part of the country that your local bookshop does not stock, you may purchase on-line.

For further information, trade, or author enquiries please contact us at the address below:
The Francis Frith Collection, Unit 19 Kingsmead Business Park, Gillingham, Dorset SP8 5FB.
Tel: +44 (0)1722 716 376   Email: sales@francisfrith.co.uk

See Frith products on the internet at www.francisfrith.com

FREE PRINT OF YOUR CHOICE
CHOOSE A PHOTOGRAPH FROM THIS BOOK
+ POSTAGE

Mounted Print
Overall size 14 x 11 inches (355 x 280mm)

TO RECEIVE YOUR FREE PRINT

Choose any Frith photograph in this book
Simply complete the Voucher opposite and return it with your payment (to cover postage and handling) and we will print the photograph of your choice in SEPIA (size 11 x 8 inches) and supply it in a cream mount ready to frame (overall size 14 x 11 inches).

Order additional Mounted Prints at HALF PRICE - £19.00 each (normally £38.00)
If you would like to order more Frith prints from this book, possibly as gifts for friends and family, you can buy them at half price (with no additional postage costs).

Have your Mounted Prints framed
For an extra £20.00 per print you can have your mounted print(s) framed in an elegant polished wood and gilt moulding, overall size 16 x 13 inches (no additional postage required).

IMPORTANT!

❶ Please note: aerial photographs and photographs with a reference number starting with a "Z" are not Frith photographs and cannot be supplied under this offer.
❷ Offer valid for delivery to one UK address only.
❸ These special prices are only available if you use this form to order. You must use the ORIGINAL VOUCHER on this page (no copies permitted). We can only despatch to one UK address.
❹ This offer cannot be combined with any other offer.

As a customer your name & address will be stored by Frith but not sold or rented to third parties. Your data will be used for the purpose of this promotion only.

Send completed Voucher form to:
**The Francis Frith Collection,
1 Chilmark Estate House, Chilmark,
Salisbury, Wiltshire SP3 5DU**

Voucher for FREE and Reduced Price Frith Prints

Please do not photocopy this voucher. Only the original is valid, so please fill it in, cut it out and return it to us with your order.

Picture ref no	Page no	Qty	Mounted @ £19.00	Framed + £20.00	Total Cost £
		1	Free of charge*	£	£
			£19.00	£	£
			£19.00	£	£
			£19.00	£	£
			£19.00	£	£
			£19.00	£	£
			* Post & handling		£3.80
			Total Order Cost		£

Please allow 28 days for delivery. Offer available to one UK address only

Title of this book . . . .
I enclose a cheque/postal order for £ . . . .
made payable to 'Heritage Resource Management Ltd'

OR please debit my Mastercard / Visa / Maestro card, details below

Card Number:

Issue No (Maestro only):   Valid from (Maestro):

Card Security Number: Expires:

Signature:

Name Mr/Mrs/Ms . . . .
Address . . . .
. . . .
. . . . Postcode . . . .
Daytime Tel No . . . .
Email . . . .

Valid to 31/12/26

Free Print – see overleaf

Can you help us with information about any of the Frith photographs in this book?

We are gradually compiling an historical record for each of the photographs in the Frith archive. It is always fascinating to find out the names of the people shown in the pictures, as well as insights into the shops, buildings and other features depicted.

If you recognize anyone in the photographs in this book, or if you have information not already included in the author's caption, do let us know. We would love to hear from you, and will try to publish it in future books or articles.

An Invitation from The Francis Frith Collection to Share Your Memories

The 'Share Your Memories' feature of our website allows members of the public to add personal memories relating to the places featured in our photographs, or comment on others already added. Seeing a place from your past can rekindle forgotten or long held memories. Why not visit the website, find photographs of places you know well and add YOUR story for others to read and enjoy? We would love to hear from you!

www.francisfrith.com/memories

Our production team

Frith books are produced by a small dedicated team at offices near Salisbury. Most have worked with the Frith Collection for many years. All have in common one quality: they have a passion for the Frith Collection.

Frith Books and Gifts

We have a wide range of books and gifts available on our website utilising our photographic archive, many of which can be individually personalised.

www.francisfrith.com